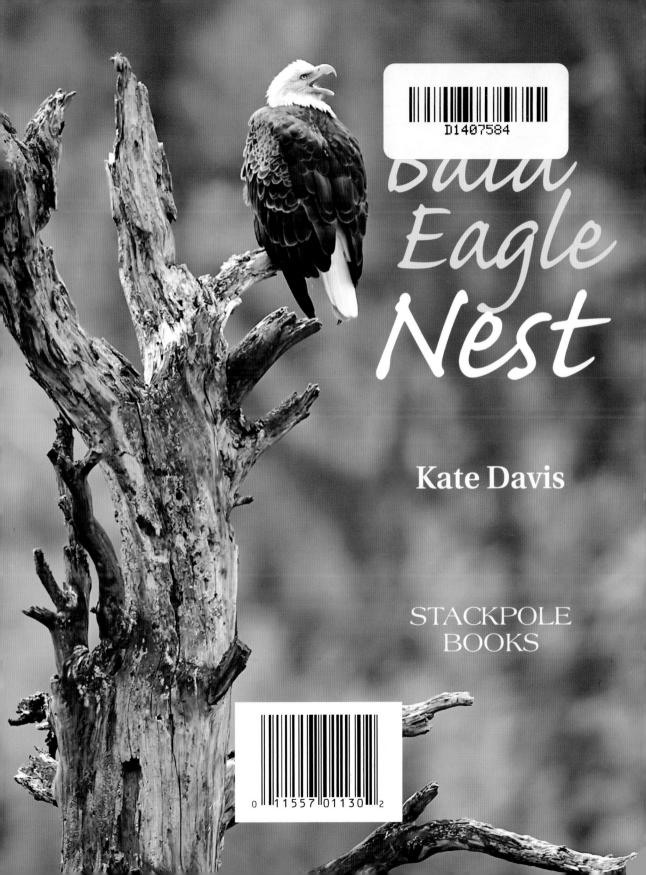

Bald
Eagle
Nest

Kate Davis

STACKPOLE
BOOKS

Published by
STACKPOLE BOOKS
5067 Ritter Road
Mechanicsburg, PA 17055
www.stackpolebooks.com

Printed in China

10 9 8 7 6 5 4 3 2 1

First edition

Cover design by Caroline Stover

Cataloging-in-Publication Data is on file with the Library of Congress

ISBN 978-0-8117-1130-2

Bald Eagles can get a bad rap.

For many, they are icons and symbols, the American Eagle with all of the mythology attached. For others, Bald Eagles are quite a different creature. Their designation by Congress as the official symbol of the fledgling United States of America in 1782 was protested by Benjamin Franklin, who pointed out that the Bald Eagle is "a bird of bad moral character" and one that often flees from tiny mobbing songbirds. Franklin preferred the Wild Turkey, "though a little vain & silly, a Bird of Courage." As Arthur Bent points out in his 1937 *Life Histories of North American Birds of Prey,* Bald Eagles may be attractive birds but are hardly worthy of this lofty place as the national emblem. He points out their cowardly and lazy habits, diet of carrion, and theft of fish from Ospreys, traits that "certainly do not exemplify the best in American behavior."

But the family of Bald Eagles I watched throughout 2011 in Montana belies that bad reputation. Both parents were superb providers, patient and thorough at feeding time, and nearly always lingering somewhere in the background with a keen eye on the enormous nest in a Ponderosa Pine. Their offspring almost seemed polite, allowing siblings to feed, waiting their turn, rarely scrapping as young birds. This in itself would make for interesting observations, but what sets this nest apart is that it fledged four young! Only a handful of known nests have pulled this off, a remarkable feat for a raptor that is often used as an example in explanations of fratricide—larger young outcompeting and even deliberately killing their smaller nestmates. Four young in a Bald Eagle nest is very rare and it seems to be a fairly recent phenomenon.

I had been photographing this nest for several years. The nest is a thirty-minute drive plus a ten-minute walk from my house, and the owners of the land it's located on are great friends of mine and allow me exclusive access. My observation point was ideal: I stood on a railroad grade, out of danger from the frequent trains, with permission from the Chief of Security and Safety at Montana Rail Link. Just beyond the tracks is an interstate highway with four lanes of traffic racing by. Traffic on the river on the other side of the nest picked up over the summer, with a flotilla of rafters and tubers floating by. So between trains, traffic, and boats, these birds were accustomed to activity and noise.

At first I was worried that my presence might affect nesting, leading to agitation and prolonged parental absence that would jeopardize the health of the chicks. But the family went about their daily activities, unperturbed by the photographer on the tracks, and later, on the beach below.

In April of 2011 I sighted four downy heads peeking out from the nest, and I staked out my spot. That first day, within twenty minutes, the male flew in right over my head with a delivery of fish. I was hooked. Over the next four months, I grew to greatly admire and respect this family of enterprising and successful eagles. This was a one-of-a-kind experience—and I have attempted to capture it for these pages.

A sight to excite—two Bald Eagles stand out against a backdrop of conifers, perched in their favorite snags over the Clark Fork River in western Montana. In 2011, this pair accomplished the very rare feat of raising four young to fledging (leaving the nest).

The huge stick nest in a Ponderosa Pine has been added to every year since it was first built in 2001. To the south and down a steep bank lies the Clark Fork River; on the north side is a railroad grade and track, power lines, four lanes of interstate highway, and a housing development. Even with all of the hustle and bustle, this nest is a local secret of sorts, easily overlooked.

In this part of the country Bald Eagles are year-round residents. Montana's eagle population grows for several months each year as birds from Alaska and Canada migrate south and settle in for the winter.

The scientific name for the Bald Eagle is *Haliaeetus leucocephalus*. The genus name, *Haliaeetus*, means "sea eagle." There are eight species of sea eagles, or fish eagles, worldwide; not surprisingly, fish is their favorite food. The Bald Eagle is truly a North American bird, with a range stretching from Alaska and Canada south throughout the United States. Some Bald Eagles even winter in northern Mexico.

The species name, *leucocephalus*, means "white head" and really only applies to adults. The individual above is about two and a half years of age, and is soaked and dripping wet after flying in a rainstorm.

Bald Eagles have been federally protected since 1940. However, persecution by the fishing and fur industries in Alaska led to the killing of more than 120,000 eagles; two dollars were paid for each pair of eagle feet in a bounty that was repealed in 1952. Eagles in the lower forty-eight states were spared bounty hunting but were still shot and poisoned, plus suffered another hardship due to pesticides starting in the mid-1940's.

At five or six years of age a young bird molts to the white head and tail and is sexually mature. The adult bird's white head also gives rise to the Bald Eagle's common name, which comes from the old English word *balde,* meaning white.

Golden Eagles like the one pictured at left are "booted eagles," with feathers on their legs all the way to the toes (feathered tarsi). They are thought to be the most highly evolved members of the hawk family; Bald Eagles have a more "primitive" ancestry nearer to kites. Immature, brown Bald Eagles are often mistaken for Goldens.

This nest fledged three young in both 2008 and 2009, which seemed a remarkable feat at the time. Then in 2011 it fledged four young. In Bald Eagles' entire range, about a dozen nests have been documented to fledge four: they are located in Virginia, Pennsylvania, Maine, Maryland, and Montana. Montana holds the record for a single state, with this nest bringing the total to six: three on the Yellowstone River (1983, 2001, 2006), one on the Missouri (2005), and one thirty miles upstream from this nest in 2008.

The eagles' neighborhood on the Clark Fork River is quiet in the fall with little recreational river traffic. The nest upstream fledged four chicks in 2008 but blew down the next year. With the Bald Eagle population increasing by nearly 10 percent per year, researchers are wondering when the numbers will plateau; they believe that the species has become more tolerant of human activity in many areas.

Mating is usually a raucous
event, with heads tossed back
and loud shrieking vocalizations. The
male briefly perches on his mate's back—
extremely carefully with those dangerous talons—
and their vents (claocas) briefly touch. They will mate
hundreds of times to produce one clutch of eggs.

　　Tales of eagles mating in the air are fictitious. What the eagles are
actually doing is courting, or in the case of two birds twirling in the air with
feet locked, fighting over a mate. Spiraling downward, such battles often part
impossibly close to crashing to the ground.

In late April, a neighbor with a spotting scope trained on the nest was astounded to see what looked like four downy heads looking quizzically about. The female attended to brooding duties as winter lingered all month, with frequent snow squalls and high winds.

Eggs are laid one or two days apart and incubation begins with the first, so young hatch "asynchronously," or in the order the eggs were laid, after a thirty-five-day incubation. Young are born with eyes open and covered in down (semi-altricial).

The first chick to hatch is the largest, a few days older than the next sibling in line, and is usually the first to be fed. Even though the males are smaller than the females, they develop faster physically and behaviorally.

Youngsters need nearly constant attention for the first few weeks, as they are unable to stay warm on their own (they are not homeothermic) until they are about fifteen days of age. Adults brood the young, warming them with their body temperature of more than 105 degrees Fahrenheit and shading them from the hot sun. The male shares these brooding duties to a lesser extent to spell the female.

As the snow from a spring squall is melting, the diligent male flies in with a sucker, a type of "rough fish" not valued by anglers. It must have been snagged in shallow water, as suckers feed near the bottom of the river and Bald Eagles just pluck fish from the surface.

The oldest chick awaits a feeding. The usual number of young in a nest is two or sometimes three, and competition for food is fierce, especially if the adults are having a tough time finding provisions. The youngest bird in a nest quite often starves to death in the first month.

As predators at the top of the food chain, Bald Eagles once consumed high levels of the pesticide DDT and its derivatives concentrated in fish. The pesticide weakened the eggshells and made hatching chicks nearly impossible, and eagle populations plummeted. Only twelve pairs of Bald Eagles were breeding in the entire state of Montana in the mid-1970s.

Peregrine Falcons suffered a similar demise. More than six hundred captive-bred falcons were released to replenish populations in the state, but Bald Eagles in Montana made it back on their own, with their numbers increasing to more than five hundred nests in 2011. The banning of DDT in 1972 and strict protection of birds and nest sites were their tickets to success.

Pairs of eagles remain together all year, with just a few months not dedicated to nesting activities.

The eagles nesting here over the last ten years may have been a single pair, as Bald Eagles are long-lived; the oldest recorded individual lived twenty-eight years in the wild. Eagles tend to be monogamous and may mate for life if they are compatible. However, if one is killed, a "floater," or unmated adult, may move in right away to exploit the opportunity.

Pigeons are constant companions on the railroad tracks, nesting under a nearby bridge.

Perhaps the pigeons did not choose the best nest site, as one of them is arriving at the nest here in the form of a meal. The highly maneuverable pigeons can out-turn a giant eagle in flight and escape, so this one was probably caught on the roost or nest—or stolen from another bird of prey that can catch pigeons, like the Peregrine Falcons that nested nearby.

Waterfowl are often part of the Bald Eagle's diet, especially in the winter when lakes and rivers freeze and they may be caught on the ice. These Mallards may have felt safe living in open water below the nest all spring and summer, as the Bald Eagles had other, more attractive food sources during these months.

The female is offering her young a Mallard head pulled from the depths of the nest. Food scraps often remain in the nest instead of being pitched over the edge. This may keep marauding mammalian predators that smell decay around the base of the tree from becoming a menace.

The mother opts to eat it on her own. Although eagles are able to catch birds the size of a goose or heron in the air, small ducks would pose a challenge because of their aerial prowess and speed. These might be domestic birds from the golf course less than a mile away, which are not as wary and may be pinioned and unable to fly.

Pieces of young Canada Geese were a favorite delivery item for several weeks, with white down flying as it was plucked by a parent. Un-flighted young geese would be easy prey—especially the goslings at the golf course. A groundskeeper reported geese being grabbed by the eagles, with the adults hunting in tandem. Once a golf ball was picked off the fairway, apparently mistaken for game!

European Starlings are also Montana residents. Here one shares a favorite perch with a Bald Eagle. About eighty to one hundred of these non-native birds were introduced in 1890 and 1891 to Central Park, New York City, to acquaint Americans with the bird mentioned in Shakespearean plays. Today an estimated 200 million live in North America from coast to coast.

One fewer European Starling in the world, thanks to the male Bald Eagle. This prey item was a surprise, and one can only guess at how it was captured. The starling was dispatched in just a few gulps by one of the nestlings.

Eastern Fox Squirrels, a regular prey item all spring, were also introduced in the area, probably so a midwesterner who moved to Montana would feel right at home with the familiar mammals nearby.

At six weeks of age, the young are able to tear much of the food apart on their own, though the parent birds still offer morsels. At this point all four are probably safe from deadly sibling rivalry, which can occur when an older bird kills the younger one or when it starves the younger sibling by taking all the food for itself.

Columbian Ground Squirrels abound throughout the valley across from the nest. Although young squirrels would be easier to catch, the ones in these photos appeared to be adults, maybe stolen from a hawk or secured as roadkill.

Another Columbian Ground Squirrel is brought in, perhaps hunted from a perch or caught in coursing flight over the colony, through the element of surprise.

Often the adult eats a portion of the prey, like a fish's head or the organs of a mammal, before bringing the rest to the nest. These may be favored parts, or the parent may be trying to lighten the load of a large prey item.

The male delivers a fish, perhaps one taken from a local Osprey (sometimes called a Fish Hawk). This is a common occurrence and some Ospreys are very reluctant to drop their catches, often leading to long chases.

Nest maintenance, which goes on all summer, includes additions of materials like this mistletoe as well as grass, moss, and the occasional stick. The castings, or pellets, of the young—indigestible material of bones, fur, and feathers that are coughed up each day—are mostly discarded over the edge or carried away.

A clump of grass is added to the nest. When the parents depart they may cover eggs or youngsters with nesting material to hide them from predators or for additional insulation in frigid temperatures.

The young are about seven weeks old now (May 30). A week after this photo was taken, a huge Black Bear climbed up the tree at dusk and tried to access the nest. The female stood her ground on a limb overhead while the male flew at the bear for an hour or more as it grew dark. Thankfully, all were safe and sound the next morning.

As with nearly all raptors, the female Bald Eagles are the larger sex, about 25 percent heavier than the males. This is called "reverse sexual size dimorphism" and may be related to the female taking over most of the nest defense during the early stages of nesting.

Both parents are feeding the young—one has brought a mammal and the other a bird. The size difference is apparent when the parents are side by side (here the male is on the left).

A Great Blue Heron stands on what is usually an island on the Clark Fork River. A record snowpack over the winter led to high river levels; the high runoff and murky waters made hunting for fish especially difficult for several months.

The spring floods inundated all of the banks in 2011. This Canada Goose is standing in a foot of water in late May in a grassy patch below the nest. The patch was submerged by rapids a day later.

An Osprey family just downstream—probably an occassional source of fish for the Bald Eagles—had nested on a platform installed in 2007 at a nursing home for residents to enjoy; a web-cam was added two years later. The muddy, turbid river water made fishing nearly impossible, and the male Osprey was forced to travel to ponds, creeks, and high moun-tain lakes to find fish.

Ospreys have a diet of 99 percent live fish, which are captured in plunges below the surface, often from a hover above. The female even joined in the search for food after the eggs hatched, leaving the nestlings unattended—a dangerous practice. Unlike their neighbors the Bald Eagles, just one of the three Osprey chicks survived. Curiously, both of the adults sport the dark feather "necklace," a trait usually reserved for the females.

A mile away as the crow (or eagle) flies is a Peregrine Falcon cliff nest, or eyrie. Unlike the Ospreys, the Peregrines were unhindered by the flood as they primarily catch birds in the air. Some of their prey may have ended up in the eagle nest after a persistent eagle forced the Peregrine to drop its prize.

Both parents now spend much of their time away from the nest, with one or both often in a snag across the river keeping an eye on things. After a morning feeding, the young sack out, hunkered down for hours. Here a mammal bone is offered to the oldest.

Despite their skills at tearing their own food to bits, the four patiently await some viscera pulled from a fresh squirrel, offered by the male. The parents often eat at the very end of a feeding bout, swallowing squirrel skins, large bones, and fish tails.

Bald Eagle nests are among the largest of any bird species, with some weighing over one thousand pounds and being used for fifty years or more. All four young frequently disappear from sight in the nest, so it must be about eight feet across and three feet deep in the bowl.

A troubling sight, as the young spend a morning shredding a plastic bag as if it were food, or perhaps in play. Fortunately, it blew away in a gust of wind. Ospreys love to add human-made items to their nests, particularly plastic baling twine that can become deadly when they get entangled in it. Bald Eagles, thankfully, use mostly natural materials.

After several circuits around the tree, the male brings in part of a yearling White-tailed Deer, the two back legs attached by the pelvis. Reports of Bald Eagles killing livestock such as lambs or calves are extremely rare, although they do feed on afterbirth; it is a mystery whether this deer was killed by one of the eagles or scavenged.

Freshly caught prey or carrion, the young don't seem to care. While road-killed deer are an important food source over the winter for young and old eagles alike, the floodwaters this spring have put pressure on the parents to find something other than fish as a food staple.

Three young settle in for a morning feast, surprisingly with no squabbling or disagreements—a testament to the responsible parents' ability to provide enough food for all since hatching. This is a formidable task, seeing that these young are nearly the size of the parents already.

Finally the fourth nestling appears interested in the deer. Biologists believe that the reason to have that third (and very rarely fourth) offspring in the nest is as a guarantee that at least two will survive to fledging for "recruitment," replacing the parents in the population.

Two nestlings play tug-of-war with a piece of deer meat while another spends about fifteen minutes attempting to swallow an oversized chunk. The following week, one nestling took an hour to swallow an entire deer tail, fur and all.

The male leaves to bring back a third deer leg; the female would appear an hour later with the fourth. The legs remained in the nest for a week with the hooves appearing now and then, poking out like sticks over the edge.

Eagles wait five or six years to breed for the first time, but then they continue to breed over a long lifespan. They invest considerable energy in raising just a few young each year. Many birds (like European Starlings) have an opposite reproductive strategy— lots of offspring per year with high mortality and short lives.

Living on the edge, a family of Eastern Fox Squirrels also inhabits the decade-old nest, appearing now and then to explore, emerging from the little cavity on the lower right where they have a nest of their own.

Two young squirrels come close to one of the eagles, and all three seem equally curious. The little rodents probably can't know that it will be months before this bird makes his first kill, and the eagle might not recognize them as having been a big part of his diet all spring.

The squirrel family was apparently perfectly at ease living in the same tree as the eagles, remaining in the Ponderosa Pine well into the autumn months.

A nestling toys with a fox squirrel skin while exercising her wings. Prey items constantly appeared in the nest out of nowhere, hinting that it was lined with butchered prey—and certainly the associated odor. Like nearly all birds, eagles have a poor sense of smell, but the insects attracted to the animal remains may be bothersome.

An Osprey attacks a Bald Eagle from above and behind, and an aerial battle begins. Bald Eagles and Ospreys are archenemies, and their fights are sometimes fatal. The odds are stacked against the smaller Osprey.

The eagle has the last word as the Osprey returns to whatever he was doing a few minutes before. Unprovoked attacks on Bald Eagles by Ospreys have been observed regularly lately, with the Ospreys sometimes diving vertically like falcons.

A squirrel leg is offered to one of the oldest youngsters. The size difference between the male and female nestlings is noticeable at this point; these two are a week apart in age and the female is larger than her brother.

The nestlings' growing flight feathers emerge from sheaths of collagen, preened open with their beaks. Two separate molts of down are replaced by flight feathers beginning at week two or three, and contour (body) feathers at week three or four. The downy feathers swirl around the nest and are carried away in wind gusts.

The abundance of food provided to the young all spring is astounding, considering the floodwaters all around them and the resulting poor fishing. The largest and most aggressive gets the lion's share of food, but competition among these four was minor—until the fledging stage.

At about fifty-two days of age, play has become an important daytime activity for the nestlings. They make false attacks at objects and siblings as they develop dexterity and muscle coordination. One of the nestlings and a parent yank a bone back and forth, a makeshift toy.

The parent is preparing to feed the youngest of the clutch some prey remains retrieved from the nest. The canopy of limbs above provided ample shade all summer.

By early July, floodwaters are subsiding and more fish are available. The male was especially adept at pulling fish from the water, finding dead ones, or securing them from other sources like theft from Ospreys or other Bald Eagles, acting as a "kleptoparasite."

Fish offer a huge caloric benefit, more so than mammals, and became a staple of the nestlings' diet.

Bald Eagle adults have the white head and tail and upper and lower tail coverts that make them unmistakable. The young may pose a challenge to identify, and are sometimes mistaken for Golden Eagles, as they undergo four or five molts before attaining the signature markings.

The brilliant white plumage of the Bald Eagle aids in defending their territory, serving as a warning to would-be usurpers. The bright plumage also signals sexual maturity; brown youngsters posing no threat to adults are treated with less hostility if they happen to fly through another eagle's territory.

Exercising their pectoral muscles, the young birds spend an increasing amount of time flapping and hopping, often in winds that could sweep them away. Their flight feathers are still growing, and the molted down sticks to the nest. Some Bald Eagle young remain in their nest stronghold as long as ninety days after hatching, but eighty days is typical.

The oldest nestling enjoys a bout of exercise while the youngest accepts an offering by the parent—another squirrel leg.

The story of "The Flying Deer" went viral on June 18, 2011, appearing in papers across the world and on the Internet. The body of a fawn was discovered draped over a power line near the nest, causing an electrical outage in town that lasted over an hour. While there were plenty of jokes about deer with wings, apparently one of the Bald Eagle parents had lost its grip on the fawn while heading back to the nest. Most of the carcass had already been eaten by other scavengers or by the eagles, but with just the legs, spine, head, and skin remaining, it still weighed an estimated twenty pounds. PHOTO BY NORTHWESTERN ENERGY LINE WORKER RYAN GIBBS

One day later, the female apparently killed a White-tailed Deer fawn across the river (she can be seen feeding on the fawn in the lower left of this photo). The young are resting in the nest, oblivious to the very fresh prey that soon will begin arriving in small deliveries.

The eagle must have launched from a favorite snag above, killing the fawn in the brush behind the Douglas-firs. She then dragged her meal to a log out in the open as the male observed from the tree in the top right of the photo. All the while the doe continued making brazen charges, stomping and flicking her tail.

The female eagle attempts to place the fawn on a downed tree, but to no avail. The fawn is larger than a newborn, and too heavy to move intact.

The perfect scavengers, magpies move in to sneak bites. The doe, now very unnerved, kept approaching closer and closer, coming within twenty feet of the carnage. After an hour she finally gave up, retreating back into the timber.

The female makes a delivery of viscera to the nest. The young eagles are ravenous, wildly flapping at what is perhaps their first food of the day. Aggression among siblings is more commonplace now, at about ten weeks.

The female Bald Eagle with another food delivery in her beak; in the meantime the male has brought in a squirrel, so the young suddenly have a stockpile of mammalian food. The male later took his turn feeding on the fawn for twenty minutes.

The partially eaten fawn was left on the hillside across the river, with both parents often perching in favorite snags on either side of the carcass. The magpies continued their feast, and Coyotes more than likely showed up that night.

Slow, powerful wing beats characterize Bald Eagle flight. Females of the northern United States have an 8-foot wingspan and weigh on average 11½ pounds (the largest, in Alaska, are up to 14 pounds) and the males 9¼ pounds. They are the second-largest North American raptor, after the California Condor.

Restless nestlings crowd a space that would more typically contain two or perhaps three youngsters. Claustrophobia must be setting in, especially with three or four all exercising at once.

Magpies are opportunistic neighbors, often robbing tidbits from the eagle nest. Like their cousins the crows and ravens, they may even break the eagle eggs if a parent leaves during incubation. Lewis and Clark wrote as they entered Montana, "more bald eagles than we have hitherto observed; the nest of these last being always accompanied by those of two or three magpies, which are their inseparable attendants."

While one eagle explores the limbs to the side of the nest, her siblings birdwatch, gazing at a magpie to the left. Magpies had fledged from a nearby nest over a month earlier, begging from the parents for weeks, just like the eagles will soon do.

Bald Eagle nestlings can increase in body weight by 180 grams (over 6 ounces) per day, reaching their highest growth rate at about forty days. They hold the record for any North American bird in daily increased mass.

All four eagles await another food delivery in a rare moment of calm
(and a rare moment with all four showing their faces at once.)

June 23 (about seventy-five days since the eggs hatched around April 10) was the last day that all the young remained in the nest together. The big female left first and perched nearby in a snag downstream.

Just out of the nest, the big female has the dark brown plumage that will fade over the summer in the sun. All of these feathers have grown quickly and all at once over the nesting period, so they are relatively weak and easily fray with wear and tear. Her feathers in the future will be stronger, with fewer growing at a time; these molts last more than six months.

A newly fledged bird appears confident in a high soar about four hundred feet over the river. This first set of wing and tail feathers is the longest the eagle will grow in its lifetime; second- and third-year flight feathers are shorter, with a complete molt of all the feathers taking several years. Wing tips of young-sters appear more pointed than in subsequent years.

Juvenile eagles have a dark gray or nearly black beak and cere (the skin around the nostrils), which will gradually change to bright yellow by their fourth and fifth years.

Several days after the oldest birds have fledged, the others are getting adventurous, exploring the Ponderosa Pine. Eagles leave the nest before feather growth is complete and build up their muscles in rudimentary flights.

Parent birds may encourage the remaining nestlings to fledge by cruising the territory carrying game or, in this case, a tree branch, which a friend jokingly remarked might be used for a smack, signaling "time to go."

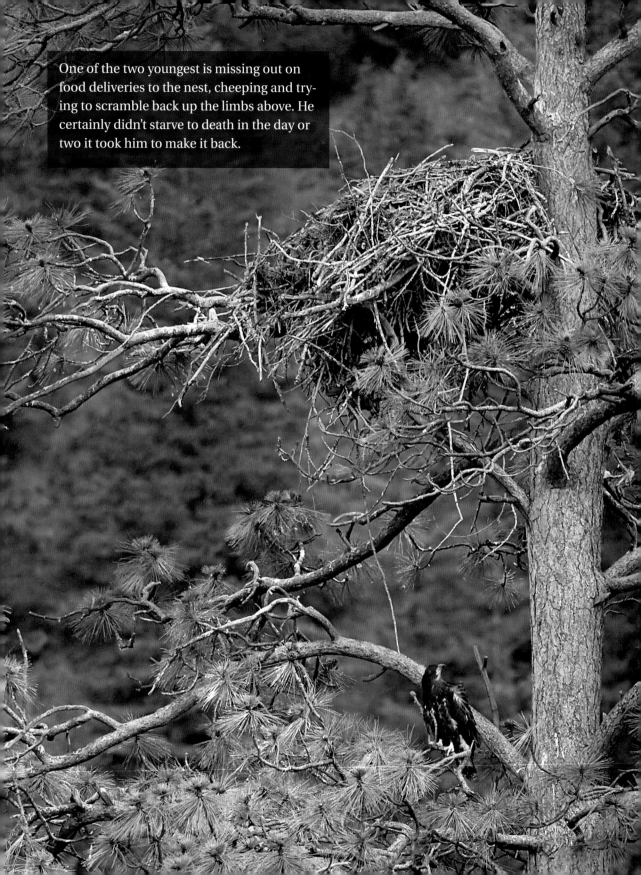

One of the two youngest is missing out on food deliveries to the nest, cheeping and trying to scramble back up the limbs above. He certainly didn't starve to death in the day or two it took him to make it back.

The male feeds on a fish close by—awfully tempting to the two still in the nest. For years this ancient Ponderosa Pine relic, dubbed the "scenic snag," has been a favored spot for young and old eagles alike.

Giant birds that often outweigh their parents, the fledglings really have no predators to worry about at this stage. Their days are spent along the riverbanks whining for hours, waiting for a feeding.

Though the nestlings are skilled at flying, landing is a different story. After this young eagle took off from a cottonwood tree he barely slowed down before crashing into the hillside across the river. That unsophisticated finish will be perfected in the following weeks.

Fledged birds in Montana hang out with parents and siblings for about four weeks, and sometimes as long as ten weeks, before dispersal. This first year is critical, as over half of the birds won't make it to year two—the tough life of a raptor. Most won't make it to adult plumage, but as adults they have a far lower mortality rate, perhaps just 5 percent per year.

A pair of Bullock's Orioles are ever-present neighbors to the nest. This female's plumage is much duller in color than that of the conspicuous male. These birds weigh a whopping thirty-seven grams (about the weight of twelve pennies) and played havoc with the fledged eagles.

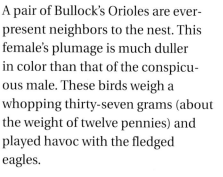

The oldest female fledgling is fairly confident in flight at this stage, perching quietly on the scenic snag. Then in come the orioles. At first, the fledgling is mildly amused. This mobbing behavior by songbirds is usually reserved for nest defence, but in mid-July the fledged orioles have been on their own for some time.

The bright orange male oriole finally gets a rise out of the eagle, who responds with a weak little scream.

The female oriole seems particularly perturbed and repeatedly bounces off the big predator. As if hinting that she has better things to do, the eagle scans the river.

Enough is enough: The eagle leaves to fly upstream, finding a calmer place to soak up the sun and wait for another food delivery from her parents.

At twelve weeks, the last eagle to fledge has only been out on his own for a few days and has never ventured far from the nest.

After a clumsy landing on the snag, the youngster tries to regain his composure, hopping back and forth on the top.

The pesky orioles start attacking, without ever letting up, and the youngster flees in frustration (or in terror), swooping through the top of a nearby cottonwood tree.

The female oriole is after him like a bullet. In his haste the eagle
almost swallowed a small tree limb.

Still bouncing off the eagle, the oriole continues her harassment. The oriole knows it can outmaneuver the huge bird and feels safe from his clutches.

The tiny oriole finally turns and heads back to the snag. The eagle must not have realized that he could simply open his mouth to dislodge the leaves, since he made repeated grabs to remove it with first one foot, then both.

Finally safe and with the leaves dropped on the beach, the eagle lands downstream and takes some drinks from the river. The orioles continued to harass the eagles for weeks to come, often appearing out of nowhere in fearless attacks.

A fledgling relaxes in the shade. The eye color changes from this dark brown color to chrome yellow by the fourth year, with the white head and tail plumage appearing the following year and signaling that the bird is now old enough to breed.

As the term "eagle eye" suggests, Bald Eagles have exceptionally acute vision, able to see detail at great distances. How are they at viewing objects close up? Obviously just fine, judging by this adult's look of curiosity at a large insect just off his beak.

Adult Bald Eagles always look dignified when perched, seeming to spend hours a day deep in thought. Somewhat less glamorous is a congregation of eagles on a road kill, often a hazardous habit that leads to vehicle collisions when the eagles have difficulty taking off in flight after gorging and try to use the road as a runway.

Her confidence increasing, one of the females launches off a power pole downstream. She is more adept at flying, and especially landing, than in past weeks. Still, the fledglings continue to rely on their parents for food and routinely return to the big nest.

The fledglings rest after chasing a parent over the river and across the train tracks and highway. The fledglings haven't hunted on their own yet, but soon the parents will discourage begging and say, "Get a job," in their own way.

A fledged eagle looking for the parents is a common sight now, much to the delight of observant floaters on the river.

The slotted last primaries at the wing tip look like six fingers. Eagles have seventeen secondary feathers, more than most other birds.

Launching from a tree over the Clark Fork River, the adult is in full fish-hunting mode. The water is finally clear after months of high runoff made it difficult, if not impossible, to secure this favorite prey item.

Trout anglers need not feel that eagles are competitors, as most of the birds' fish diet consists of suckers, whitefish, pike minnows, catfish, and non-native carp.

A fledgling frantically chases after a parent with a fish. The plumage with a spattering of white on the ventral (abdominal) side and tail is characteristic of a young Bald Eagle. Size is no way of telling the two eagle species apart in the field, but habitat might be a clue: Bald Eagles rely on water, while Golden Eagles favor remote open country and typically nest on cliffs (with some in trees and others on the ground).

An adult Golden Eagle has overall brown plumage, and a smaller head, neck, and beak than a Bald Eagle. In a soar, they show a "bulge" on the trailing edge of the wing, and hold their wings in a slight dihedral (a shallow V).

In November, with the cottonwood leaves turning, the adults remain together. Nesting activities will resume in the following month and into January, starting with courtship and nest repairs.

Bald Eagles were delisted from the Endangered Species list in 2007, and populations in Montana are probably at a record high. Nonetheless, most people can't help but pause, if only for a moment, to take notice of such a spectacular creature.

The Bald Eagle voice is a weak "ki-ki-ki-ki-ki-ki-ker" reminiscent of a gull's call—an unexpectedly minor vocalization from such a large bird. The call of a Red-tailed Hawk, apparently more impressive than the eagle's, is often erroneously swapped in films and television.

Now on their own, the young eagles face human challenges of power lines, traffic, and trains. Tragically, one of the females was struck by a vehicle on the highway nearby a month after leaving the nest, and later died at a rehabilitation center, after earning the nickname "Snapper" for her attitude in captivity.

An adult launches in the last rays of sunlight in December. The young have dispersed and are on their own, perhaps somewhere on the Clark Fork, Blackfoot, or Bitterroot Rivers.

In December, the eagle nest looks uninhabitable. However, after some repairs, another clutch of eggs was laid the last week of February; the saga continues.

Once a rare sight, these magnificent birds have made a comeback, and are as impressive as ever. Despite the bad rap they get from some people, these predators are worthy of respect as rulers—or ruffians—of the waterways.

Many thanks to:
  Dick and Christine Everett
  Pete Lawrenson, Montana Rail Link
  Sam Milodragovich, NorthWestern
    Energy

Ryan Gibbs, NorthWestern Energy
Carmen Bassin
Sue Erickson